Dreams of a Psychopath
A Long Poem
Saumitra

Translated By- Dhiraj Singh

Copyright © Saumitra Saxena & Dhiraj Singh
All Rights Reserved.

This book has been self-published with all reasonable efforts taken to make the material error-free by the author. No part of this book shall be used, reproduced in any manner whatsoever without written permission from the author, except in the case of brief quotations embodied in critical articles and reviews.

The Author of this book is solely responsible and liable for its content including but not limited to the views, representations, descriptions, statements, information, opinions and references ["Content"]. The Content of this book shall not constitute or be construed or deemed to reflect the opinion or expression of the Publisher or Editor. Neither the Publisher nor Editor endorse or approve the Content of this book or guarantee the reliability, accuracy or completeness of the Content published herein and do not make any representations or warranties of any kind, express or implied, including but not limited to the implied warranties of merchantability, fitness for a particular purpose. The Publisher and Editor shall not be liable whatsoever for any errors, omissions, whether such errors or omissions result from negligence, accident, or any other cause or claims for loss or damages of any kind, including without limitation, indirect or consequential loss or damage arising out of use, inability to use, or about the reliability, accuracy or sufficiency of the information contained in this book.

Cover Painting Credits - Safdar Shamee

Made with ♥ on the Notion Press Platform
www.notionpress.com

For Waheeda Rehman, and

In memory of Firaq Gorakhpuri, Gajanan Madhav Muktibodh, Naresh Mehta, and Guru Dutt

All the children snatched away by the wars of men.

1

I am a dreamer
And I dream
Was I wrong?
People used to say
All sorts of things about me—
'The Brain', Thinker, Philosopher
Dislocated from the real world
Chasing after something
Amorphous, something that exists only
In the realm of ideas
A rare and magnificent creature
A tireless speculator
Of the mind.

And I would
With a heavy heart
Take these labels
Showered on me
In my stride
And immerse myself
In a strange strain of
Romanticism.

In those moments
Of reflection
I would investigate

DREAMS OF A PSYCHOPATH

My hidden talents
Sit down before a mirror
For hours
And gaze upon
Each part of my
Winning self
With trembling lips
Holding back a thin and ethereal smile
Of self congratulation.

These eyes of mine
That can feel
And fondle my
World-conquering dreams
Are but a small
Part of my body—
How deep they are
When you gaze at them
You realize they
Have in them
The sublimest and
The saddest scenes
From the whole universe
Are hidden in their cavities
As tiny layers
Scattered around
Drunk
With I don't know what
Kind of worldly wisdom
That snatches sleep
From the eyes of the wise

With a mere blink
And possesses each atom
Of their spirit—
Because I am too
Searching in them
The sky
Of my own romance
Sometimes.

In this process of
Admiring myself
When I descend from the eyes
And reach the forehead—
Whoa! The shine
Dazzling with the gleam
Of seven suns
This temple of mine
Is like a dot of
Brilliance—
Exuding rays of light
From the mischief of dawn
To the gloom of dusk
Containing everything
From celestial space
To the space between things
The greatest manifestation

The most magnificent mound—
With those fine ridges
Just look at them
Radiant like mountains,

DREAMS OF A PSYCHOPATH

Valleys and cave networks
Formed on the sun
After a solar storm.

Still lower
I spot a fair and glowing
Face like one carved in stone
With a pleasing and well-formed nose
Whose valleys rise over the cheeks
And lips
I admire nervously their
Unmatchable movement—
How a slight inward pull of the cheeks
A pout of the lips
As if chewing
Can put me in the hall
Of fame of history's
Finest philosophers!
And when they laugh
I turn protector
Of the entire world's oppressed—
As if I am saint or
A messiah or a prophet.

Then another feeling
Would take hold of me

And I would leap
Through the layers of my body
To admire
My inner

Construction—
The first thing I would
See would be
My heart
Delicate beyond words
Like thin glass
It would shatter on touching
Despite being packed
With the stories of a generation
Tied to me—
Worried
Battling, bearing, weeping, tormented
Absorbing every bit
Of pain from this world.
Not broken by a stone
Swung at it
But splintered by
An on-purpose
Looking away—
It has many soulful
Parts like the loneliness
Of a girl still looking for a boy—
Spotless, innocent
And full of soul, my heart!

By the time I reach my spirit
I would've thought a lot
About Its being in this world
And its historical impact—
The important twists and turns
Its being has caused in history

Both classically and definitively
On this world
Through me—
I would think about that.

Then I would stand up
Straight and hold my right finger
In the air and
Brace my left hand to my side
Looking ahead like
The Statue of Liberty
In New York
Giving a new message
To mankind
Or
Perhaps, sitting
Legs folded together
Below the knees
Bald and naked above the waist
A penurious brown shape—
The world's most famous
Activist making cloth
On a spinning-wheel
A Gandhi dwarfing
Everyone else
I would've thought a lot
About Its being in this world
And its historical impact—
The important twists and turns
Its being has caused in history
Both classically and definitively

Construction—
The first thing I would
See would be
My heart
Delicate beyond words
Like thin glass
It would shatter on touching
Despite being packed
With the stories of a generation
Tied to me—
Worried
Battling, bearing, weeping, tormented
Absorbing every bit
Of pain from this world.
Not broken by a stone
Swung at it
But splintered by
An on-purpose
Looking away—
It has many soulful
Parts like the loneliness
Of a girl still looking for a boy—
Spotless, innocent
And full of soul, my heart!

By the time I reach my spirit
I would've thought a lot
About Its being in this world
And its historical impact—
The important twists and turns
Its being has caused in history

Both classically and definitively
On this world
Through me—
I would think about that.

Then I would stand up
Straight and hold my right finger
In the air and
Brace my left hand to my side
Looking ahead like
The Statue of Liberty
In New York
Giving a new message
To mankind
Or
Perhaps, sitting
Legs folded together
Below the knees
Bald and naked above the waist
A penurious brown shape—
The world's most famous
Activist making cloth
On a spinning-wheel
A Gandhi dwarfing
Everyone else
I would've thought a lot
About Its being in this world
And its historical impact—
The important twists and turns
Its being has caused in history
Both classically and definitively

On this world
Through me—
I would think about that.

Then I would stand up
Straight and hold my right finger
In the air and
Brace my left hand to my side
Looking ahead like
The Statue of Liberty
In New York
Giving a new message
To mankind
Or
Perhaps, sitting
Legs folded together
Below the knees
Bald and naked above the waist
A penurious brown shape—
The world's most famous
Activist making cloth
On a spinning-wheel
A Gandhi dwarfing
Everyone else
Surface-less ghost planet
Of your imagination.'

That broke my heart
So bad that
I stopped dreaming
For good

DREAMS OF A PSYCHOPATH

I began to starve
The psychopath in me
Bit by bit.

And my romanticism—
Once of a dreamer
Had become that of
A psychopath.
The story that day began
In the evening breeze
As I ran my fingers
Through her hair
Entranced,
Enraptured
For a few moments.
She was stuck to me
Like a branch on a tree
Her head resting on me
Listening with intent.
I was going to tell her
My dream
The one because of which
She left me.

'You know, darling
I am a great thinker
So let me tell you
A dream I dreamt
Last night in which
I saw a glimpse
Of the entire

Universe.'
Half asleep
Half awake
Senseless—
Thoughts randomly colliding
With each other
As in Brownian fluids
A scene emerges—
Mount Rushmore
In the USA
Humungous
With four faces
One of them familiar
Toasted golden, leaps
From its rocky cage
He is the great Lincoln
Or is it me?
I am not sure.
When he becomes
Fully human
They surround him
Thousands and thousands of
Black men
Who were made
Slaves.
Tortured and half-dead
Hungry, naked
Broken in their prime
Countless
Men, women, children!
The Lincoln that is me

Inspires them
To battle arms with ideas.

My dearest countrymen
Let's join our hands
Together and declare
War with these
Naked and lifeless bodies!
Get up and write
Your future with your
Own hands,
Come!
The time has come
To wipe out this
Slavery
This empire of colour
That trades humans
According to their skin.
The time has come
For a political order.

Peace!
Like a TV screen
Pixelating
Without signal
Breaking into a screaming
Dance of static.

A new image
Takes shape again—
On Indian soil

Somnath's awesome temple
Surrounded by hideous Turks
With flowing black beards
And eyes of fire
Galloping towards it
In waves.
Flushed-faced
In the melting heat
Comes Ghazni
Shouting to his troops:
'Trample them
Destroy them
Smash their idols
Erase the infidels
From the face of the Earth.'
I am the only one
Standing
I am a priest
Exhorting my people
'Fight!
Till there is blood
In your veins,
Turn the sea red
With the blood
Of the Turks!'

I am alone
Helpless when
A sword cuts off
My head
And I watch

With the eyes on my
Severed head
The destruction
Of places of learning
Of places of worship
Indian heads crushed
Under Turkish boots.

The scene changes again
A peculiar silence
That stretches
From the curtain of the lashes
To eternity
A desert
Perhaps the Rajputana.
Look!
At the funnels of dust
Struggling for a way out
Of the dry scrubs
And the tip-tap of horse hooves
Giving way to the sound
Of sinking camel feet.
It looks like an army
Soldiers rushing
From one end of the earth
To the other—
It's Alauddin Khilji
The Sultan of Delhi
Perhaps he going to Chittor.
And there is Ratan Singh—
He is me—

He is about to roar
And then fall silent
The evil Sultan will gaze
At Padmini in a mirror.
Come, let's prepare
Call all the girls
For the Jauhar
All women: babies,
Young ones, mothers and grandmothers
Without fear
Embracing the giant
Flames of the
fire pit
Of Jauhar.
It is a brave time
I am Ratan Singh
Standing before Alauddin
Sword in hand
It is over
For there is only ash
The Sultan is beyond angry
He orders my killing!
But I am alive—and how?
Let's talk about
Something less
Blood-boiling
Sleep is falling over me
Perhaps some
Other scenes
Are looking for me.

DREAMS OF A PSYCHOPATH

I see rivers
So long that
They reach the ends
Of the earth
Sphinx, pyramids, caves and huts
Deep forests
Deserts, melting heat
Rain, sea
A voice in the background says
'This is Africa
And that is Algeria—
I am holding a pen
When I enter
What am I doing?
I am writing
But what?
I am writing about
Reformation
Against orthodoxy
A nation steeped
In bloodshed
And acid rain
In the name of religion
Spread all over
Devouring me
Bit by bit.

What is this?
What have I walked into now?
Looks like Uganda
What kind of monumental

Rage is this?
The dead are all over
On the streets
In thousands
While Washington is
Preaching through the
Loudspeakers
I scream: 'At least cover these
Naked dead bodies!'
What kind of stink
Is this? It is from
A neighbouring country
Where the skeletons
Are piling up
From hunger and disease
What is this country?

Somalia, Ethiopia or Sudan?
What's in a name anyway?
I am battling
The collective harvest
Of minefields— where the crop of death is reaped.
Epidemic here
I'm like a mother
Am suckling a baby
Skeleton in my lap.

I fly
I reach Europe
What kind of conference is this?
'One Currency For Europe'

DREAMS OF A PSYCHOPATH

Famous faces are hobnobbing
Dreaming of a
United economic power
But they don't notice
The place where my eyes
Are fixed
Serb strongmen
Violating
Muslim women
Infants, girls
These are wars
With no end
And they're
Against women
Of all kinds.

I jump in
A shimmering
Sword in hand
'Don't you dare touch
them, you bastards!'
I fall again
Defeated
Staring at my own martyrdom
But my work here isn't done—
I have to stop
The acid-throwers
Of Afghanistan
Who throws acid on faces
Of girls without veils.
I have to stop them

Before their faces
Are disfigured forever.
I have to stop
The fire from spreading
On the streets
Of Karachi.
What kind of world
Is this?
Where there's no one
Besides me who
Cares about these things.

I return to India
Prime Minister's Office
South Block
All the secretaries
Are standing smugly
One of them says aloud:
'US Foreign Secretary
Ms Madeleine Albright has
Stated that Kashmir
Is an integral part of India.'
The Prime Minister
Looks pleased with himself
I barge in screaming—
'Have you no shame?
Is America your father?
Telling you what is
And isn't an integral part
Of India!'

DREAMS OF A PSYCHOPATH

A lot is happening outside
There's pandemonium
Then there's silence
One part makes noise
While the other stays silent
Then they change places
And so it goes
I have truly arrived
In my country
So many people
Posters with faces
All over
It's like a conference
Of wolves
And the topic:
Soft lambs are
Hard to find these days!
So we have to soften them
Make them more
Persuadable
Again, which is
very doable.
I'm carrying something
In my hands
As I wander
Near Rajghat
The residential colonies, bylanes
And the slums, yes
I am selling handkerchieves
'Perfect for tears!'
But there are no buyers

Rage is this?
The dead are all over
On the streets
In thousands
While Washington is
Preaching through the
Loudspeakers
I scream: 'At least cover these
Naked dead bodies!'
What kind of stink
Is this? It is from
A neighbouring country
Where the skeletons
Are piling up
From hunger and disease
What is this country?

Somalia, Ethiopia or Sudan?
What's in a name anyway?
I am battling
The collective harvest
Of minefields— where the crop of death is reaped.
Epidemic here
I'm like a mother
Am suckling a baby
Skeleton in my lap.

I fly
I reach Europe
What kind of conference is this?
'One Currency For Europe'

Famous faces are hobnobbing
Dreaming of a
United economic power
But they don't notice
The place where my eyes
Are fixed
Serb strongmen
Violating
Muslim women
Infants, girls
These are wars
With no end
And they're
Against women
Of all kinds.

I jump in
A shimmering
Sword in hand
'Don't you dare touch
them, you bastards!'
I fall again
Defeated
Staring at my own martyrdom
But my work here isn't done—
I have to stop
The acid-throwers
Of Afghanistan
Who throws acid on faces
Of girls without veils.
I have to stop them

Before their faces
Are disfigured forever.
I have to stop
The fire from spreading
On the streets
Of Karachi.
What kind of world
Is this?
Where there's no one
Besides me who
Cares about these things.

I return to India
Prime Minister's Office
South Block
All the secretaries
Are standing smugly
One of them says aloud:
'US Foreign Secretary
Ms Madeleine Albright has
Stated that Kashmir
Is an integral part of India.'
The Prime Minister
Looks pleased with himself
I barge in screaming—
'Have you no shame?
Is America your father?
Telling you what is
And isn't an integral part
Of India!'

DREAMS OF A PSYCHOPATH

A lot is happening outside
There's pandemonium
Then there's silence
One part makes noise
While the other stays silent
Then they change places
And so it goes
I have truly arrived
In my country
So many people
Posters with faces
All over
It's like a conference
Of wolves
And the topic:
Soft lambs are
Hard to find these days!
So we have to soften them
Make them more
Persuadable
Again, which is
very doable.
I'm carrying something
In my hands
As I wander
Near Rajghat
The residential colonies, bylanes
And the slums, yes
I am selling handkerchieves
'Perfect for tears!'
But there are no buyers

Or maybe they have no money
Or perhaps
Their tear glands
Have dried up
Then I reach
Parliament House
My mouth fills up with
Vile abuses
I pick up a stone
But the security men
Catch me and throw
Me in a jail
Where I become
Another 'custodial death'.

The scene changes
It is the last
Watch of the night
The heart is murmuring
I am on the edge
Slightly crazy
Seeing the image
Inside my head—
'Darling, isn't that your picture?'
I feel as if I have
Found you after
Living through the
Hells of this life—
And you've come
To give me comfort
And your soft touch

DREAMS OF A PSYCHOPATH

A film song plays
In the background—
'My love, come to me
Come into my fair arms
Why are you sad?
Why are your lips dry?
And your eyes longing?
Why my love, why?'
I am lost in Lata Mangeshkar's
Melodious voice
As my head gets
Lighter on your thigh
With the strokes
Of your tender fingers
On my forehead.

My pain is lifting
I am feeling
Tipsy with a
Realization that you
Are with me
A few lines, written
Some time ago as fiction
Are becoming real
Like our dreams—
'When your eyes turn to mine
When they stop searching
For light in a dark maze
When a downward gaze is
An admission of love and
A chain that binds a sweet

Dream from end to end—
This is the mirror of my eyes
Dear friend
If you scratch my face
It's the mirror that will bleed
It's not your usual mirror
Of cheap stones
That cannot capture
The marks of epiphany.'
I repeat these words
To myself and then I am
Overtaken by a
Romantic rapture.

The scene changes again
A face begins to emerge
Flickering like
A reflection on water—
It is Guru Dutt
Yes, the same one in
'Pyaasa', 'Kaagaz Ke Phool' and
'Saheb, Bibi Aur Ghulam'
The father of poetry in cinema
Guru Dutt, the crazy poet
Born star-crossed
Searching for the
Waheeda of his dreams—
For the ultimate
Romance—
Oh, that is not Guru Dutt
That is me!

DREAMS OF A PSYCHOPATH

You! You!
Where are you going,
Waheeda?
I will die
I will kill myself
My inner romantic
Wants to live!
Oh God
Please give the gift
Of romance
To those inhabiting
This Earth
Make them forget
All their miseries
Their small-minded
Battles and clashes
Their living for some
And dying for others
This is the sky
The highest point
A slice of love
For every philosophy
Of the world.
A slice of love
For everyone!

Suddenly there is
A shower of stars
It makes my spirit soar
As if I have found
The answers to all

The world's problems.

Come
Drop everything
The slogans of bread and hunger
Slaves listening to Lincoln
Come here fast
Villagers fleeing Ghazni
Come here
Come Ratan Singh
Padmini you too
The young of Africa
Women victims of genocide
Come
The dead of Karachi
The fakirs of India
Come in pairs
Come holding each others' hands
You too, Guru Dutt and Waheeda—
Come celebrate with us
With me and my lover
This moment in history
This moment
Without strife
Struggle, desolation, loss and death
This moment of love
A slice of love
For everyone!

I wake up
Stand up straight and ask:

DREAMS OF A PSYCHOPATH

'So darling, this was
My dream, the soul
Of my ambitions
Did you like it?'
I wait, hoping
For an answer.

But there's absolute silence!
Maybe, she says:
'Psychopath!
Mental!
In your telling
There is only you
And you only
Despite the crowd
Of heroes
And villains you've gathered!
Search your soul
Find out where
You're wrong–
You've worn a victim's
Torn hide
Now you're looking
For a salve.
Go, find yourself. Goodbye!'
I am stumped
I have no answer.
Thinking about everyone
Has reduced me
To half, not
Enough to stand up

To her as a full person.

2

She leaves
I'm not broken
Fallen as I have
From the moon
This is not the whole
Truth.
I have lost sight
The connection of dreams
Is lost
All corners of my mind
Are screaming
Angry words
Then a thought comes to me
Perhaps I should stop
Flying and floating around
And come down to Earth
Perhaps I should only
Take small leaps and
Reach out for the sky
Of my romanticism.

This is my curse
A black mark
The mockery of my hopes
I wish I could hiss aloud
With a raised hood in anger

But my lips quiver
My arms flail
My feet tremble
And my steps falter
As I walk and
Soothe my ambitions.

'Life, I am coming
To live you fully
I am on my way, darling
To prove to all
My endless
Self.'

It is a tar road
Houses made of brick, stone and concrete
This is a human dictionary
I search in it for those
Who need me or do they?
Is there anyone who
Shuts his eyes to God
But calls out to me!
How do I tell these people
Today, I am not that
Buddhist monk who's out
On a journey
Of a lifetime.

The scene changes
I am seized by a feeling
Of overwhelming motherliness

DREAMS OF A PSYCHOPATH

It is a street
In a familiar town
I have seen him
A million times
Near the rail tracks
Where old carriages are left
At bus depots
In the city and the outskirts
Street corners and highways
Near garbage dumps
He is there always
Today he's letting
Me feel sorry
For him
Wholeheartedly without interruption.

A filthy man
Near a heap
Of broken glass, rusted iron and polythene bags
Is looking for meaning in garbage.
I am overcome with emotion
Why is this man losing himself
In meaningless things
I want to tell him:
This is not life
Snatching bread from
Dogs around
Heaps of garbage
I know it sounds poetic—
These seldom-mentioned
Words become poetry

In these situations—
I say to him:
'Friend, I want to live
A part of your pain,
I know, water doesn't stick
On lotuses
And that there is no heat
In the moonlight
And him whose fate
The sun handed over to
Dawn isn't worried
And him whose heart
Has become a pustule
Of sadness has no one
To cry for him
But himself
That's why I want to
Give you company
The one thing missing on the face
Of this Earth
I want water to stay
On me, I hate
Those heartless lotuses
I want to light your
Dead flame and take
Away the darkness
From around you.
I want to live
A part of your pain.'

I wake up startled

DREAMS OF A PSYCHOPATH

What kind of fantasy-dream is this?
I think I have stumbled again
Down some rabbit hole
I am like a madman
Why am I telling all this
To an animal
Like it's going to
Change things?
But surprise
This creature speaks
Like a human
Is he human?
And then I begin
To hear him clearly.

'My friend,
My fellow traveller!
(He hands me his bag
Full of trash)
You talk of relieving
My pain
Of filling my life with light—
But even I know this
That the sun rises everyday
And night too falls daily
Who can end
The darkness?
Who's been able to trade
Someone else's
Commotion and wrinkled brow
I am eating what I have sown

This is my battle
Let me live my struggles.

It is baffling
His assault on my feelings
And my efforts
How can he be so foolish?
Then I take hold of myself
And begin to explain to him
The principle of my compassion
And my romanticism.

'But life is not like that
Just wallowing in the dirt
It is about soaring
With your thoughts
And your dreams.
You think we don't hurt?
We don't dream of
That one someone
On whom we
Can shower all
Our love?
Come on, you can do it
Search yourself
Scratch the surface
And you will find it,
Perhaps a little less
Perhaps none at all
Perhaps,
The biggest romance

Of your life.'

Just then it all changes
He begins to cackle:
Laughter like the
Roar of clouds
He laughs and laughs
Unstoppably
So much that his
Dirty eyes
Begin to rain
Big fat drops
Of salt water
All around him.

His terrifying laughter
Stops after what seems
Like ages
He goes silent
His mouth curls
His eyes become stony
And his body trembles
A pitiful smile
Forms around his mouth
As if he's not looking at me
But a child whom
He's out to humour.

'My friend
I used to hurt too
Somewhere between

The highest flights
And the deepest depths
I too feel the prick
Of darkness
Of our breaths,
And the tug
Of light
Of my dreams.

When I bang my head
Against the mausoleums
Of trash, carrying
With me the weight
Of skipped steps
Across abandoned nights
In the inky desolation
Of the sky
When I shove my hands
In the pits
Of the charnel ground
Made of glass and poison
To pull out flavours
Of stale bread
It hurts me too
There where men
Stand and piss
My eyes too tear up
With anger when
I am pulling out
Hate from the ground

Below these walls.

My friend
Those whose passports
Of fate have mentioned
In them—a few naked kins,
Some on-sale sisters,
Knowingly, unknowingly
The burden of handicapped
Mothers and fathers.
Those without
The benign glance of
A caring friend,
Folks like them
Have no choice
But this.

Am I really human?
As I search for God and space
In the empty parts of the city
Where light goes
Dark on reaching
The edges,
The broken horizon
Made of iron rods,
Tin sheets and
Rolls of paper.

My friend,
I don't ask anything of you
Except that feeling

That I can read
In your eyes
That your will not
Hold me in contempt
And that you will not
Frighten me.'
Saying this he walks off
Carrying his bag of rags on his head.

I am stunned
Speechless
With bloodshot eyes
I am numb
I've witnessed the murder
Of my romanticism
I have just now seen
Two filthy hands
Strangle the love
In my heart
Yet I am whole
A thought rises
A picture forms
In the centre of my eyes
As if I am still walking
After being hit by a train
I am alive
I keep walking.

Damn!
Where have I reached
Scary desolation

DREAMS OF A PSYCHOPATH

Silence that barks
And tries to bite you
Black clouds are pouring
Rain and turning the night
Even darker
I have lost my way
Faraway from the settlements
Of the rich—
These have to be the ruins
With spiders, bats, snakes,
Brick, dust and
Peeling plaster,
Falling roofs and
Towers that stand
In silence.
I get scared
Where has this gotten me?
This running
From myself
Fighting myself
Just then I hear the wails
Who's this I wonder
Whose voice has pierced through
The sheets of silence:
A cry in the wild?
Who? Why?
Is there someone with me
In this desolation
Some luckless fellow.
Maybe it is a child.
Yes, it does seem like that!

I panic and my feet
Rush toward the sound
Falling, stumbling,
Falling and getting up again
I reach there and find
Lying there in the muck
Injured by sharp stones, thorny bushes
A baby–
Screaming
On top of the universe.

I am overwhelmed
By this vision
Of terror and destiny
'I will save him'
I tell myself
'let me be your saviour
My young friend'
I pick him in my arms
Tenderly
I try to rock him
Imagining the countless
Marys who have rocked
Their babies in a manger.
Then bang.
It feels as if I've been shot
In the head
I fall to the ground
But I am not dead
I am back on my feet
Seething and bleeding

DREAMS OF A PSYCHOPATH

And then I see her
Standing behind me
A woman seething
I get it now
I get the full picture
I feel her pain
My anger disappears
And in its places
This hitherto hidden
Greatness that I
Squeeze into my voice
And I say:

'Sister, who are you
Running away from?
Bringing yourself at
The gates of hell
And not just you
But an innocent
Baby too?'

There is silence.
She doesn't know
Where to begin
I notice her face
Is covered.
She is cold under her wet clothes
Shivering
In the silence
I can hear heartbeat
Duk, duk, duk, duk

She says nothing
So I keep talking
'Are you looking
For somebody?
Why do you seem so sad?
What have you lost
Is it family, home?
Or has some monster
Violated you?
Is it? Tell me, please
He has sent me
The one who looks after everyone
He's sent me to show
You the way
To give you a new life
Look at me...'

Even before my
Words are uttered
They are lost
In the wilderness
Stuck like
Drops of candle wax
In my ears.

'I am a whore
I have been kicked out
From my job, from your pleasure dens
The mirror too turned against me
Showing me my wounds and my sores
When I became a mother

DREAMS OF A PSYCHOPATH

It has been my biggest curse
I have tricked death
To reach this place.'

She screams and grabs
My shirt collar
'You man, why don't you
Buy me or better still
Kill this child
Do that thing that I
Can't bring myself to do!'
I feel I am being tested
For greatness, I become resolute
And shout back:
'I will not buy you,
You sell yourself
So cheaply and cheap...'

A strong gust of wind
Takes the clouds away
Letting the moonshine
Her veil is off too
I scream in terror–
Her skin is burnt to the bone
And boils cover her neck.

Her body shivers and
She lets out a shriek
'I knew you wouldn't
Bring yourself to pay for me
Then let us perish here.'

I am lost for words
'But... I... I didn't mean...'
'Let me fight my own battles'
I am lost for words
As she fades away
Into the darkness with her child
I fall like a eucalyptus tree
Crackling at the base.

I remain lifeless
On the ground
My mind, blank
Like a blank slate
And then after some time
I wake up with new energy
As if a moment ago
I hadn't felt like dying.

And then it comes back
The same scene
Making me question
My convictions
The ashes are slowly
Popping new embers
Half-baked promises
Big waves of romance
Are beginning to rise
In my mind's ocean.
'How can my love
Be defeated

Like this?'

My beloveds—
My fellow travellers,
My fellow flyers,
Fellow inhabitants,
Compatriots
I am coming
To free you
From your struggles
To take you to
The pinnacle
Of your romance—

This is a new town
But it seems familiar
Ancient, medieval
And space-age
All civilizations are scattered
There is a road
And a bacteria-cluster of men
On the side are
Settlements of polythene,
Sack-cloth and cardboard
Near which are dumpsters from hell
Containing human pieces
That are wailing, coughing
And making agonizing sounds
Then laughing
Like madmen
Naked armies of children

Foreheads branded, condemned
To a life
In rags
Like loose buttons of a shirt
Running-scrambling, huffing-puffing
I don't know what
Keeps them up, those faces.

And then I slide
Into a crossing
A masked traffic cop
Exercising his hands
With watchful eyes
Cars whizzing past
Foreign-made
Swank as
The white, shining faces inside
Like mollycoddled sons-in-law
Of life
Living it up
At their in-laws: the world
Blowing smoke from Marlboros
Lipstick sticking on the butts
Fingers snapping and
Pushing the button
Of the car stereo
And a western star
Starts yodeling.

There are bicycles
And scooters too

DREAMS OF A PSYCHOPATH

Sloppy men
And fashion men
Everybody's in a race
Of horses, horse-carts, bullock-carts,
Tempos, rickshaws, trucks
I don't know where to go
A red-light stares at me
This is my last chance
Of today's journey
Who will listen to me
My philosophizing
Who will be interested
In my life?
See, my dear
Am just trying to walk
I scream—am just trying
To give you a good show
Like a ring-master.
'Hey friend, stop
Please hear me out!
Please let me change your mind
For the sake of humanity.'
They surprise me
As they stop
But why?
I don't think I have
The looks to make them stop
Perhaps they've stopped to see
This entry-free show
Of someone coming under a bus
Or not

Because they begin to listen
To me intently
Perhaps taking me to be a seer
I am over-joyed
A crowd begins to gather
The richest
And the poorest
Men and women, old and young
They all surround me
and I begin to tell them
About my
Philosophy of love.

'My friends
Look deep into my eyes
And try to read
The dream-lines drawn in them—
Forget your daily race,
Your daily struggles
Leave everything and
Search in them
A few moments
Of love and romance.
The best medicine
Of all the world's ills
Is romance.
Romance with that emptiness.

This is no infatuation
Of two young and eager hearts
It is instead

DREAMS OF A PSYCHOPATH

A life-giving stream
The art of giving up
Everything for
Love.

A mother's giving up things
For her child is her romance
A sister's affection
For her brother
Is the romance of human bonds
A father's slap on
His errant son's face
Is the romance of duty
To make sacrifices for
A friend
Is the romance of loyalty
The romance of the stomach
Is bread
The romance of naked bodies
Is dressed in rags
The romance of kids of a coughing mother
Is in a cough-syrup bottle
The romance of martyrs
Is the hangman's noose
The romance of a worshipper
Is a stone idol
The romance of a soldier
Is the border
It is also bursting mortar
The romance of collapsing dreams
Is a body flying

From the force
Of a bomb explosion.

Another name
For romance is the crashing
Of the ocean's waves
Against rocks on the shore
Voices—yours and mine
Swooping down thousands of feet
Into a mountain valley
And coming back as an echo—
Is the romance of nature
The easterly lifting
The veil off a new bride
Is the romance of playfulness
Of the wind
And the clouds
In the sky bursting suddenly
And wetting the Earth
Is the romance of thirst
For life
The living and the lifeless
Man and rock
Everything is made
To be spent
On something else
I have come to be a merchant
Of this kind of romance
I have left her behind
For whom I could give my life
'Everyone should have

DREAMS OF A PSYCHOPATH

Someone like that
A love of his life
A someone for everyone
This is the greatest philosophy
Of all time!
Come, let me begin
By making this declaration—
Get me all your woes
Your struggles, bring them to me
And I will live them
And die your deaths
I will be your guide and philosopher
I will sow my dreams
In your waking eyes.'

And then murmurs begin
In crowd that's listening
To me transfixed
Did I say something wrong?
Did I betray their confidence?
That suddenly my words
Have begun to have
No effect on them
Where did I lose them?
If not as a guide
They should at least
Accept me as their
Fellow human
Stupid, dumb, gullible people!
I shout at them:
'Wake up and recognize

Your guide and protector
Feel my grace!'

The signal turns green
Endless engines roar to life
The endless grind of life
Begins again
There is an old man, limping
Perhaps he will tell me
But he too is going back.

'Sir, why are you all running away
What crime have I committed?
How did I lose you all?'
He hesitates, trembles
Like a lamb being
Petted by the butcher
And says in a voice shaking
With fear and old age:
'Let us be, O saviour!
Please just let us live
Our own
Sorrows and struggles!'

I am utterly disappointed
So I yell at him
'Why do you want
To live your struggles?'
The old man steadies himself
As if after a huge shock
And then replies calmly

'A good desire
Expressed wrongly,
A good story
With a bad ending,
The right philosophy
With a wrong footnote
Search yourself
Push and pull and stretch
The layers of your mind
And you will find your answer.'

Wordless, thoughtless, lifeless
All desires gone
All resolves abandoned
This is the final blow
And it seems to have worked
I have lost, I give up
All my defenses are at your mercy
Dear life!

3

I was a dreamer
And I used to dream
It is one more
Of my illusions
Because the dreams
Still haven't left me

Come back
Please return to me
My lost self
My romance
Your suffering maniac
Is calling you

My voice returns to me
As a battered echo
Slammed and banged
Against every piece of rock
Shattered and wailing
It embraces me
As I stand at the edge
Braving the winds and the clouds
Alone with my feet
Firmly on the ground.

There is no grand statue here

That's standing for centuries
In the heart of a glorious nation
In a legendary city
And neither is there a voice
Of great literary repute here
That tells of things
Of humanity.

I am tired
I sit down
Embracing my knees
Fists tightened
Head bowed till my chest
Face contorted
And body breaking.

But no one can see
My misshapen shape
The small, darkish skinned
Saviour of the world
Who has turned the universe
Into a child covered in dust

No one remembers
A half-painted Monalisa
Inside the soul
Below the heart
Is stretched a flame
A terrible sight
Jan Hus at the stake
Running scared

Lost in the maze of space
Is the Copernicus of the mind!

Rousseau—
Forgetting words
Pen, all over the place
Feet, faltering
Loses the alphabet
Einstein is tied up
In naked electric wires
His time is bad
Space-time is contracting
The switch is turned on
Current races from his veins
To the heart
A fuse is blown
His story ends.

The mirror looks different—
Has the image changed or
Has the man?
I look closely—
I want to meet myself
Again and feel
The remains of that
Earlier world.

Pursed lips
Holding back fear
Lips chafed and cracked
Bleeding from the corners—

DREAMS OF A PSYCHOPATH

The eyes see it
And flinch taking in
The scenes
Layer by layer
One by one
As if peering down
One endless chasm

And then a landslide—
Mountains crumbling
With deafening sound
The white snow on them
Makes a face.
Isn't that me?
But where are the others?
I cannot sleep
My spirit, stunned and panting
Like a scared animal
The sky has shifted
I have reached the depths
Of my romance
My feelings
Dashed to the floor.

The stains have escaped
And stuck to my forehead
The darkness is like
The blackness of space
The blackness that comes
After the light star
Has shifted

When the sun has gone rogue
And taken all light
Like a black hole
That pulls everything
And leaves only desolation
Stuck on the forehead
And yet all-engulfing.
I come down
My face is no more rigid as stone
My skin is like glass
Something cracks
Unmarked like the sky
I come down from the pits
To the mountain-tops
I silently admire
The shape of my
Lips and cheeks
How their trembling
And their turning pale
Puts me in the category
Of the weakest man
In the entire history of man—
In search of saviours
Messiahs and
Prophets.

I climb the walls
Of my physical self
And I wander
In search of that
One thing that I have

DREAMS OF A PSYCHOPATH

Left behind
Close to my heart
The thing that was
Tender beyond description
Like the finest glass—
Now shattered to pieces
Only the echoes remain
Of fading tales
Told by my heart:
Now heavy, crying, screaming in pain
Shattered to pieces
Alone in the whole, wide world.

I move ahead and dwell
Upon my spirit
The point in my
Personal history
Where I'm struck
By a classic tragedy
Formless and scattered
Like an endless chaos
Of criticism
Then the mirror screams—
Where are you?
O' famous
And uncommon
Philosopher
Thinker
Philosophizer of everything!

I am about to fall asleep

About to lose
Consciousness
I am asleep now
But wait, something's happening
Is there no peace even in sleep?
What is this?
Looks familiar
Like a best friend
Is it a dream?
Yes, it is
I can feel it—
There's something different
The setting of the stage
Is different
Black curtains over the eyes
Some blurry images
Undefinable
What are they?
A mass of hungry, black and naked people
Innumerable
As if a swarm of locusts
Has descended
A man is standing
He is the same Lincoln
That is me
I am saying something
About freedom and equality—
Just then the army descends upon on us
Countless soldiers
In bright, shimmering uniforms
On horses

DREAMS OF A PSYCHOPATH

Brandishing double-barrel guns
And lightning-fast whips
Swinging in the air
'Destroy them,
All these bastard
Negroes, let no one
Live.
Cut off their heads!'
Their war cries
Pierce my ears
As they speed off
Piercing men, women and children
The sky trembles
I run
Leaving it all behind
Lincoln is terrified
I am terrified
I run for cover
At last I find a mountain
And start to sculpt on it
My face, my features
Slowly I begin to turn
Into stone
Four faces are back on the mount
Someone from the present shouts
'Lincoln has become stone
Lifeless, without feeling!'
The scene changes
To another situation
It is Hindustan
The Temple of Somnath is standing

Amid a siege of
Long bearded, ruddy-faced Turks
As far as the eye can see
It is Ghazni who shouts—
'Crush them,
Remove them from the face
Of the Earth
And raze their idol-filled
Temples to the ground.'
Then he notices me—
The temple priest
I am shaking with fear
He orders his men—
'Stop and pay attention!
Let's entertain ourselves today
For a change
What do you say, O' priest!
Here, take this hammer
And break down your
Ungodly idols,
We shall see
The magic of your
Hands today
And give ours some rest.'
I raise the hammer
And rains blows
On the idol
Till it is crushed to a thousand pieces.
I am hoping that now
Maybe he will
Spare my life

DREAMS OF A PSYCHOPATH

And not throw me
Under his Turkish
Horses to be pounded
And crushed.
It all goes silent
For some time
And it all changes again
There is mist
Or maybe a dust-storm
Am I in the desert?
Yes, it is the Rajputana again
Clouds of dust
Whistling through the shrubs
Touching the skies
As thousands of men on
horses and camels
Pummel the earth
With their marching steps—
They have surrounded Chittor
Khilji is furious
Inside the fort
I am furious too—
Padmini will not reconsider
Showing herself
Even in a mirror
Ratan Singh is irritated with her—
I fear for my life
Of defeat
And total carnage—
It is making me mad
I am going crazy—

I pull Padmini by the hair
And drag her through
The corridors
The bylanes
And passages
Of the fort
People look at me
With hate-filled eyes
Some of them throw stones at me
Curse me and spit at me
As I stand
On the ramparts
Holding the queen
Like a common slave.
Ratan Singh shouts out—
'My saviour
And benefactor
O' Alauddin
Take this woman
And spare me
And my kingdom!'
The woman I am holding
Spits on my face
Pulls away from me
And leaps into the depths
Below the fort walls
To remain forever pure.
I stand there alone
Empty-handed
The pyres are lit
For the Jauhar

DREAMS OF A PSYCHOPATH

Everything is burning
Only I am left
I meaning Ratan Singh.
The scene changes again
Long rivers flowing to
The ends of the earth
Thick forests, heat
Desert surrounded by the sea—
Before someone yells
From the background
I have recognized it—
This is Africa
Again I wonder
What am I doing here?
What country is this?
Perhaps it is Algeria
The air is thick
With something sour
Acid rain!
Red roads, red walls
Red eyes, red hands
There is murder on the streets
The murder of liberty
Of freedom
Fundamentalism is on the rise
The tender-hearted are burning
God is being bullied
I run
I leave the battlefield
Who has put a pen in my hand
Who wants me to write these

Tracts of liberty
I just want to fly away
From here
And save my life.
Where have I reached
Flying?
So tired
And nose sore with the stink
Are these?
Somalia, Ethiopia, Congo, Sudan?
Hunger is shameless
What fruits can you find
In the orchards of death
Two skeletons wrestling over
A palm-size piece of flesh
Diseased, sunken-faced
On the verge of death.
I run again
Snatch the piece of flesh
From them
And smash their heads
With stone
But the hunger remains
Bullets are flying
Half-naked corpses are falling
All around
My clothes are rags now
The horrors of my travels
Have done this to me
I pull a piece of clothing
From a dead body

DREAMS OF A PSYCHOPATH

It's fully naked now
But I don't care
It is dead
And I live.
I fly again
Over the expanding sky
Now red-tinted with blood
Like the screeching echoes of
Crows cawing.
I come to Europe
I am now a diplomat
Engaged in worthless diplomacy
'A unified economy is
The answer to all our
Chronic and historic ills'
They're listening
In rapt attention—
The world's high and mighty
A thousand women scream
It is the Renaissance
A reporter wants me
To answer
And I reply grandly
'To preserve the edifice
Of our world!'
I fly
The scene changes again
I am in Hindustan
Will I find peace here?
South Block—
Prime Minister's secretariat

The secretaries are standing
As mute spectators
While I am fuming—
'Kashmir is a disputed part
Of the Indian subcontinent'
There is commotion outside
Someone picks up a stone
And tosses it at my motorcade
I am enraged
And I order my
Security men
To skin the rebel
Alive.
The scene has changed again
It is the last watch of the night
Again the heart is melting
And the mind is split
Into many, my thinking is blurry
A picture is taking shape
In the eyes (sleep fools
Me to think you're with me)
But what is this?
What clothes are you wearing?
Dressed like a Naxalite
Warrior in the jungle
With a double-barrel gun
On your shoulder
Face in disarray
Hair all over the place
Eyes red
Voice full of anger—

DREAMS OF A PSYCHOPATH

Why are you asking me these questions?
'Young friend
Stand up straight
Then lie on the ground
And act like you're
In the throes of a painful death
Like a young girl
Tortured with pain
Of an abortion
Done inside a lonely hut
In a lonely jungle!
Don't move, stay there
And now act like
A half-dead bitch
Yelping and barking
After eating one pup
From her litter
Of four
Because of unbearable
hunger.
Okay forget that
Now stand up–
And look at the scene
In front of you–
Imagine you're a helpless
Untouchable woman in a village
Naked and being chased with sticks
As your husband lies dead
From knife and bullet wounds.
Well, okay dude
Stop now

It doesn't matter
Sit down.
Now imagine you're
A mother
Whose son—a labourer
Has just been buried
Alive under a landslide
And she's looking
At his cooked and pulpy body
Weeping and singing
With the neighbourhood women
Loudly banging a tambourine,
C'mon show me her pain.
What? Sweetheart
Can't do that?
Should I tone down the tasks?
Okay, forget it
Why so serious?
Just show me this—
How a father pulls
Himself together
Drags his heavy feet
After marrying off
His daughter
Or maybe try this:
Become that girl
Rejected by 24 families
Because she's not pretty
Or maybe this:
Breakdown utterly like
Someone who's lost all hope.

DREAMS OF A PSYCHOPATH

Come on, this is your test
You have to become
Anyone of these!'
She fades away
After jolting me
I am burning with rage
I become Guru Dutt
But my poems evapourate like steam
The character has changed
Romance is disappearing
Obsession is taking its place
Waheeda! I grab her
My hands reach for her throat
I will destroy you
Or make you
Kill yourself.
Who's there?
Who is there?
Two shadows!
Whose shadows are they?
I think it's a woman
With a man's head on her lap
They're silent and
Gazing into each other's eyes
I go near them
And ask:
'Tell me, O' man
What is the secret?
What's the magic?
How do you have power
Over this woman

Have you held her
Forcefully with your hands
Or perhaps
Tied her hands and feet
Tell me how
A sublime smile spreads
Across his face
As he begins to speak.
'Love-romance
Are names of feelings
That make you want
To give up everything
For someone
To get lost in eternity
It's really a blessing from God
Someone for everyone
To live for that one
And to die too
For that one.
This is the gist
Of all wisdom
Of all philosophy
A slice of love for everyone
Everyone for a slice of love.'
My mind is in a tizzy
Scenes are colliding with each other
Repeating all that's passed
It seems I have won
Against everyone
Turned everyone into dwarves
And am now sitting

DREAMS OF A PSYCHOPATH

On the highest mountain
The earth is shaking
Under my weight
I cannot run from here
There is a bottom-less chasm here
A scary chasm
I sob uncontrollably—
I have lost everything
Trampled upon everything
What's left is me alone
I am like a tree stump
Admiring its last leaves
Falling.
Clouds rumble suddenly
Lightning cracks
The sky turns black
It is the end perhaps
Everything is trembling
Maybe it is an earthquake
The earth is turning
A new leaf
Giving my burden over
To another page.
A volcano has erupted
There is bubbling lava
The sky is melting in its heat
I am certain
I am going to die
I am afraid
Then I see someone
Who is that?

So small and defenceless
A baby eagle
It has dropped from the sky
Into my lap
Now it will also die
With me.
Tough luck!
As if by design
The heartbeat races
Why not
Do something noble
As I die
Why not try
And save this little one!
I hide its tiny body
In my coat
And shut my eyes
Waiting for my end.
It's coming
It's coming
It is right here
Very close
Beads of sweat
Ooze from my temples.
But what's this?
Why has it all stopped
Everything is back
In place
The volcano has died
The earthquake too
The clouds have gone

DREAMS OF A PSYCHOPATH

The sky is watching mutely
Then music pours in
Like a mystical chant
In the silence
Of a forest
What's that?
It is incredible
I can barely believe my eyes
What if I lose
My mind again
This is you
Like a dream fairy
Dressed in silver and gold
You're crossing the seven skies
You're coming to me
So close
Your lips begin to part
But I am speechless.
'All your life and
Its many contradictions
Are contained in
These drops
I am overwhelmed
By you again because you
Have found romance
In these drops of sweat.'
I wake up
Stunned
The dream is over
But what's this in its place?
It is all real

It is her
Before me
Smiling.

Authors Notes

SAUMITRA

A prominent figure in Hindi poetry for over 25 years, has written more than 200 poems and numerous stories, many featured in renowned literary magazines and anthologies. His critically acclaimed debut poetry collection, 'Mitra,' won the Bhartiya Jnanpith Navlekhan Award in 2007 and was translated into English by Dhiraj Singh as 'I like to wash my face with seawater' in 2020. His anthology, 'Kahin Door Jakar Dam Todane Ka Man Hota Hai,' followed in 2022. Another significant work is the long poem 'Ek Swapnadrashta Ka Romanticism,' acclaimed as an important early 21st-century Hindi poem by 'Samay ke Sakhi.' Harish Bhimani, a celebrated Indian voice-over artist, has narrated

three of Saumitra's poetry compilations. Currently, Saumitra is a scientist at a leading university in Middle-East Asia, dedicated to tackling climate change and reducing carbon footprints.
Email: saumitra.saxena@gmail.com.

DHIRAJ SINGH

DHIRAJ SINGH is currently DIRECTOR & ASSOCIATE DEAN at MIT-World Peace University's Dadasaheb Phalke International Film School & Department of Media & Communication. He is the recipient of INDIAN ACHIEVERS' FORUM's 'Man of Excellence Award-2021-22' given in recognition of his outstanding contribution to Journalism & Nation-building. He is a novelist whose first book 'MASTER O' brilliantly imagines the future where the rule of men

AUTHORS NOTES

is overthrown by a species of mutant elephants who can change physical reality. 'Master O' has been translated into Hindi owing to its critical success.

Email: dhirajsin@gmail.com